Of Earth

new and selected poems

John Daniel

John Daniel

LOST HORSE PRESS

Sandpoint, Idaho

FIRST EDITION

Cover Art: *Untitled 3—Earth & Sky Series* 48" x 60" acrylic on canvas
            by Saman Rooeintan, whose artwork may be viewed online at
            www.marstudio.com
Author Photo by Amanda Smith
Book Design by Christine Holbert

This and other fine LOST HORSE PRESS titles may be viewed online at *www.losthorsepress.org*.

Library of Congress Cataloging-in-Publication Data

Daniel, John, 1948-
Of earth: new and selected poems / by John Daniel.—1st ed.
     p. cm.
7 (alk. paper)
I. Title.
PS3554.A553O35 2012
811'.54—dc23

                                   2012026517

for Sam, Max, and Lily,

for Chris, Jon, and Eileen,

and with a nod to my eclectic trio down on the Farm,
Ken, Denise, and Simone

Contents

from *All Things Touched by Wind* | 1994

New and Uncollected Poems | 1994 – 2010

To the Reader

For this book I have gathered, in its first two sections, the poems I would like to keep from my two previous collections, *Common Ground* and *All Things Touched by Wind*. I have fiddled with many of them—more than fiddled with a few—but all should be recognizable to any who know them. The fiddling I cannot help. I seem to be a writer for whom publication is merely a change of typeface, and any typeface is markable by pen. Nothing in Nature is finished or ever will be. Why should human works be any different?

When I turned to prose in the late 1980s, my work in poetry slowed but never ceased. Every few moons I returned to the little stacks of drafts, tried again to find what might make a particular poem whole, and, if lucky, worked it a pace or two in that direction. In the last four years I've been writing a few more. Several poems in the third section of the book germinated in this recent period. Others have been evolving slowly for ten or twenty years, and two go clear back to the late 1970s. A few have appeared in magazines or anthologies, but all are "new" in that they haven't previously found print in a collection of my own.

Most of the seventy poems in this book were inspired by the landscapes and wildlife communities where I have lived or spent lengths of time over the last forty years. A good many came from the sagebrush, juniper, and ponderosa pine country of south central Oregon, particularly Langell Valley under Goodlow Rim, where I became a writer and where I still spend parts of every year. Some arose from the grass and oak hills of the San Francisco Peninsula above Stanford University, some from the Rogue River Canyon of southwestern Oregon, and some from the inland foothills of the Oregon Coast Range west of Eugene, where I have lived since 1994. Others grew out of tramps and visits here and there in the greater West—in Death Valley, the White Mountains, Baja California, Point Reyes, Joshua Tree National Park, the canyons of the Colorado Plateau, and of course the Cascades of Oregon and southern Washington.

But poems arise from multiple sources. A few of these came from dreams, two from city streets. One came from a candle, another from a photograph, another from 9/11. Some came of love, and a few of those came also of grief. Several grew out of gratitude toward mentors. Some came to me as prayers, overt or implicit. A few hark back to my anxiety over the nuclear arms race in the 1980s. One or two were spurred by environmental issues, but those concerns I have put mainly into prose. In poetry I want to touch the beauty, integrity, and mystery of the given world, which I call Nature. To celebrate that world, I believe, is as important as to decry its ruin. To celebrate it *is* to decry its ruin.

In going through these poems I've been reminded that many of them engage mortality in general or my personal death in particular. This has been a preoccupation since childhood. I could be wrong, but most people seem to have a filter that keeps fear of death mostly out of mind, through youth and midlife at least. I was born without that filter. In my twenties, when I read Carlos Castaneda's books, I tried to take to heart Don Juan's admonition to take death as one's advisor. I have worked at this through meditation, and, as I came to be a writer, through language. This colloquy with death is probably the heart of my entire enterprise in writing.

Though I never set out to be a nature poet—I've simply followed my lifelong affinity for the given world—it is fair to label me so, unless the labeler believes that nature poetry can only be pastoral idylls or admirations of scenery. "Nature" means "having been born"—microbes, humans, the entire cosmos itself, with all the living, dying, love, loss, joy, horror, beauty, and questions about ends and beginnings that the cosmos has so far evolved. Like all true literature, nature poetry belongs to the ongoing conversation the human community is conducting through time about who we are and where we have come from, about where we are and who our kinfolk are, about how we live and how we might live, about how our lives should matter.

Though I don't believe the nature of Nature can be encompassed by scientific study alone, the lenses of science are invaluable and I draw considerably on what they bring into focus. I also draw upon American Indian literatures, Buddhism and Taoism, the Christian and pagan traditions, the American Transcendentalists, and poets such as Walt Whitman, Emily Dickinson, Robinson Jeffers, Theodore Roethke, Kenneth Rexroth, William Stafford, Denise

Levertov, and many others still living. I am a spiritual and scientific generalist, intolerant only of fundamentalism in either realm. I need all the help I can find in trying to understand this Nature that is us and everything else. These poems are products of a kind of nearsighted groping toward forms of truth that can be realized, if at all, only in the process of seeking them. One name for this seeking is imagination, which is not a way of making things unreal but of trying to know their reality by calling it forth in language. My intent is that each poem should embody its portion of truth in ways accessible to the general reader. I am not interested in making clever puzzles or clouds of vague significance. My aim is to attend to the living world and make true reports.

John Daniel
Winter Creek and Pine Flat, Oregon

from *Common Ground*

1988

One Place to Begin

You need a reason, any reason—skiing, a job in movies,
   the Golden Gate Bridge.
Take your reason and drive west, past the Rockies.
When you're bored with bare hills, dry flats, and distance,
   stop anywhere.
Forget where you thought you were going.

Rattle through the beer cans in the ditch.
If there's a fence, try your luck—they don't stop cows.
Follow the first hawk you see, and when the sagebrush
   trips you, take a good look before you get up.
The desert gets by without government.

Crush juniper berries, breathe the smell, smear your face.
When you wonder why you're here, yell as loud
   as you can and don't look behind.
Walk. Your feet are learning.

Admit you're afraid of the dark.
Soak the warmth from scabrock, cheek to lichen.
The wind isn't talking to you. Listen anyway.
Let the cries of coyotes light a fire in your heart.
Remember the terrible song of stars—you knew it once,
   before you were born.

Tell a story about why the sun comes back.
Sit still until the itches give up, lizards ignore you,
   a mule deer holds you in her eyes.
Explain yourself over and over. Forget it all
   when a scrub jay shrieks.
Imagine sun, sky, and wind the same, over your
   scattered white bones.

You're close now.
Wander up a dusty ravine until your nose smells
    something different.
Climb to the green grass, the stand of aspens.
Squirm your toes in black mud, with the tracks
    of hooves and paws.
Drink. The face that rises to meet you
    has been waiting for you to come home.

For the Fire

In cold morning sun
I raise my maul, aim
for the calm pooled rings
of a round of pine.

Two halves spring from the block,
fresh-faced grain
on glaring snow. Drunk
with the dangerous musk of pitch

I swing with all the hard love
I know, slick with sweat,
grunting with the drive
of the eight-pound steel.

The split pieces settle
heavy in my arms
as I walk to the shed, dry lips
on bare pine flesh. Rough

and gentle as any father,
I stack them to sleep
for that ice-still morning
I will come to them, lonely,

asking for their warmth and song.

Reading

Reading a book on the living room rug,
I've been glancing over as I turn each page
for an hour now, and the lizard's still crouched
outside the floor-to-ceiling window, its head
tilted to the night. What's it waiting for?
No insects out there, just a few dry leaves
on bare concrete, just the October dark
and this five-inch dragon, gripping the sill
and growing stranger the longer I stare.

The rabbit's nerves I understand—we had
the same mother once, a furry something
who stayed alive through luck and jumpiness
in the fern-swamps of Tyrannosaurus.
When coyotes howl my scalp prickles, some call
of my own turns over in its sleep. Even
the birds, reptilian themselves, are bright
and soft in their masquerades of feathers,
they warm their young—

                                but this lizard's belly
must be as cool as window glass. Its blood
moves glacially. It is part of the night
some silent way I've forgotten. It's home,
it waits for nothing. I put down my book,
slide slowly across the carpet. I see
the palpitation of its waxy throat,
the splayed fingers, tensed elbows, the tail
curved on a leaf—and the blunt head flicks,

a yellow, side-staring eye takes me in.
I do know it somehow, it's an old dream
I can't quite raise. *Lizard*, I say, as if
the name could clarify, as if to stir
some answer from the stillness of its gaze,
not curious, not fearful, but aware.
We stare through glass, absorbing what we can,
each a vague trouble in the other's eye.

Why I Listen to Family Stories

When Aunt Frances sits up tall in her chair
and her eyes loom dark and huge in her lenses
and she announces it's time I got married,
"Remember your Uncle Tell," I say, and Frances
laughs like a girl—
                    because Tell Daniel made
the best harness in Missouri, but never learned
to drive his own Model T, so Frances,
six feet of schoolgirl, steered it to his shop
on the square one steamy August evening
to bring Tell home for dinner, and Tell,
a gentle man who smelled of cool leather,
said Frances should turn right instead of left—
or left instead of right, she isn't sure now,
but she's goddamned sure how she turned on Tell
with all six feet full of scorn—
                        "*You don't*
need a brain to be a Daniel, only a good
pair of ears, 'cause there's always another
Daniel around to tell you what to do."

First Light

I stand at the woodstack
with owls still calling,
four deer in the frozen pasture,
the tops of the tall pines
incandescent with sun.

This is the way it begins.
We come back to ourselves
always here, now, in the light
divided from dark by no clear line,
that returns us to our own keeping.

Could I drop these hunks of pine,
melt into morning like a coyote,
see the house, from far,
as one more thing? In this light
anywhere would be home.

The owls answer each other.
The deer watch, listen.
We are wakeful together,
as if keeping an old promise
to meet here, in this first light.

The Elm in November

The slow labor of summer
is finished, the yellow weight
delivered to ground. Twigs
jittering, buoyant with wind,
the elm comes round once more
to the grace of emptiness.
It enters the cold unburdened,
its life withdrawn inside
the solitude of its dark limbs,
exact pattern against gray sky,
the spare shape of enough.

The Sound of Mountain Water

Hiking the ridgecrest
you mistake it for wind—you know
it began long before,
a whisper that finally woke you.
Retrace the trail
till you're dead or crazy,
you won't find a line
between sound and silence.

Closer, you're sure for a moment
it called your name.
Your mind chases
slippery syllables, the fluent tongue
of snowmelt on granite
that forgets what it starts to say.
You remember camps
on other streams—you're weary,
hungry for supper.

Awake by cold ashes
you've arrived at last—
moon, pines, that naked voice.
On the trail next morning
you're so filled with its song
you forget that the stream is miles
behind. Then suddenly
you hear the dry silence.

Unidentified Critter in the Locust Tree

I heard a hummingbird
revving its motor
in the locust tree.

When I stuck my head
through the leaves
to see what kind it was,

it propped itself on air
two feet from my face,
took a good look

and flew like hell.

Note to a Young Fisherman

for Andy Hamilton

Before your rod arched
with that unseen strike
and the taut line sang
through the surface of possibility,
the ocean within you was still,
brilliant with what could be,
ready to be surprised.
You might have reeled
a mermaid from that water.

It's not the lure, it's that
glint of mind that gets the fish.
Cast yourself far from shore,
don't fear drifting in darkness.
Visions will flash from the depths.
Understanding will tug, slip away,
tug again. And someday
the one you've been waiting for
will swirl to your surface,
fighting hard as it must,
the wise and beautiful one
you somehow knew was there.

Joshua Trees

These bent trees that Mormons saw
as the prophet waving, waving the way
through desolation to a better land

I see as hunched arthritic geezers,
ballerinas, monks who've long forgotten
how not to pray, and I'd have to watch

until mice made a home in my skull
to stop seeing man—as if to be real
they have to be human, as if

these shaggy trunks, these spike-leaves
stirring in steady dry wind
showed any way except their own,

as if this rocky sand they rise from
half an inch a year, the only trees,
this soil that gives them all they need

to put forth clumps of heavy bloom,
each limbtip bursting in creamy flower,
as if this ground they're rooted in

were not itself the promised land.

Beginnings

No god broke these billions of stones,
or knows where they will be, or what,
in a billion years. No higher power
commanded cactus from the stones,

or magenta blooms from the cactus pads.
The darting hummingbird drinks *here*,
now *here*, its only map the flowers
themselves, and sparrows dip and veer

among the sharp-spined yucca trees
with precision they don't need to plan.
They find their way, as the swirling breeze
finds its own way, and the clouds

through their immensity of light,
and these are not the works of mind
but mind itself, mind waking to say
stone, cactus, flower, wind—

speaking these things, and finding its way.

A Crossing

. . . my only swerving—

—W. S.

Blinded in light the deer stopped—
my fender crumpled, hurled her
down the bank.

I found her thrashing,
the broken legs trying to run.
Pleading, hating her ruined life,
I grabbed a rock and hammered her head,
again, and again—

and stood breathing hard
in the silence of stars and pines,
smeared rock a perfect fit
in my fingers.

Again my headlights
tunnel the dark. I grip
the wheel, one of the strangers
who kill at any crossing,
without the stomach to pay dead life

the respect of an honest hunger.

A Year among the Owls

1

At dusk an owl sits blinking
in the oak
as students walk home, alone
and in pairs
through the silent quad,

lifts its tail, craps white
and flies
to the ridge of the red-tiled roof—
silhouette,
turning its head
one way then the other,

still there
as it grows too dark for me to see.

2

You can't see the owl at night,
but it sees you.

Sometimes at dusk you can see it,
but it saw you first.

In daylight you can haul yourself up
and peer in its hole. It's asleep.

You're still not important,
even though you've climbed a tree.

3

With the call of one owl the stillness
of lamplight and desk is changed
to the stillness of forest and night.
From the nest in the pine, the hollow oak,

from barns, mineshafts, seacliff ledges
they glide forth, soundless, seeing and hearing
with a clarity we could not bear, a field
of bright knowing across the dark land.

4

In the classroom we talk about our poems.
Outside in the rain
the owl in the oak and the owl in the palm
call to each other.

5

I assumed you were still
when you gave your call.
I didn't know until now,
watching you in the palm,
that your white throat puffs
like a tuba player's cheeks,
and you lean forward
very carefully it seems
placing your voice into air.

6

I am like the owl in two ways:
I sleep in the day,
I move into homes I did not build.

Some think the owl is lazy.
Some think the owl is smart.

7

Tired of reading while the owl calls,
I open the door and answer:

hoo-hoooo   hoo   hoo

It is silent the rest of the night.

8

When it comes I hope it's at night
in the fields, a sudden shadow
against stars. In the grasp
of that vision much clearer than mine,
I'll rise with my fading light
in the great silent motion of wings.

9

As I heard the owls in my sleep
I kept drifting to the surface
and downward again.
Toward morning I dreamed of a boy
blowing a song on an empty bottle,
over and over, alone
in the dark but not afraid,
trying to get it just right.

After Hearing from a Friend

Since you called, I've been walking
the wet grass listening to frogs,
their steady chorus pulsing along
until a few at a time they hush,
and hush, and the last frog chirps
kind of silly for a while and quits.

My loud footsteps, wind in the trees,
stars scattered like farmlights
lonely on the prairie . . .

are you *there?*

                      are you *there?*

are you *there?*

          are you *there?*

               are you *there?*

                      are you *there?*

—and every damn bubble-throated frog
in the meadow is chirping its heart out.

Who knows why they sing, but tonight
it sounds like celebration, tonight
I think the only reason they stop
is for the pleasure of starting again.

Return

What is this joy? That no animal
falters, but knows what it must do?

—Denise Levertov

When at one in the morning a raccoon
rustles out of the brush
and rises on hind legs peering
like a bear at my lamplit window,
swaying slightly, forelegs out-thrust,
then drops and walks its lumbering walk
into darkness, for a moment
I am wholer than before—
as if joined with the self
I am always losing, who is curious
and curiously sure, who embraces
all things in its calm regard,
never troubles itself
with forethought of death, and always
in the black light of darkness
sees its slow-stepping way.

The Longing

Death is the supple Suitor
That wins at last—

—*Emily Dickinson*

When he slipped on the mountain
I would have held him
but he chose the jolt of the rope.

When the raft overturned in the canyon
he was confused, he went up
instead of down to my arms.

I wait to the right, he turns left.
I am on time, he is early or late.
I whisper when he lies awake at night,
he turns on a light, he pretends
he does not know me.

I cannot forget his face—
every day he becomes more beautiful
and my longing becomes harder to bear.

But I wait,
I know him better than he knows himself.

I watch him walk in circles,
lift his feet in the same worn tracks.
All the time he comes to me,
like a moth in love with the moon.

I watch him read books,
scratch words on paper,
he will understand nothing
until he looks in my eyes.

I watch him build his heap of things,
find friends and lose them, couple and part,
I am the one
always beyond his reach.

I was with him in the darkness of the womb.
They took him out screaming, he promised
to come back to me.

When I step from behind that final tree
he will throw down everything, even his name,
and before we lie down together
he will hold out the handful of blood
that remains from his birth, crying *here*

I carried it all the way for you.

Of Earth

for Wallace Stegner

Swallows looping and diving by the darkening oaks,
their white bellies flashing,
the tall grasses gathering last light,
glowing pale gold, silence
overflowing in a shimmer of breeze—these
did not have to happen.
The heavy-trunked oaks
might not have branched,
and branched, and branched still further
as if to weave themselves into air.
There was no necessity that a creature should fly,
or that last light should turn
the grasses gold, or that grasses
should exist at all, or light.

But a mind thinking so
is a mind drifting from home.
It is not thought that answers each step of my feet,
to be walking here
in the cool stir of evening
is no mere possibility,
and I am so stained with the sweet
peculiar loveliness of things
that given God's power to dream worlds
from the dark, I know
I could only dream Earth—birds, trees,
this field of light where I and each of us walk once.

The Apollo 17 Photo of Earth

That shape called Africa,
that form I learned from the Rand McNally World
on my bedroom wall, wondering
How do they know how continents look,

that image the word *Africa* makes
in millions of minds, that clear outline
of a thing never seen

is how it actually is—bulging West,
straight slant of Red Sea coast,
the graceful narrowing to Cape of Good Hope,
even Madagascar, the boot of Arabia—

only now I see no puzzle of pastels
but the tawny land itself, dappled, delicate as skin,
bright Sahara disappearing
around the western world-curve,

Africa shadowed in the south
with streamers and froth of thick white cloud
swirling up from Antarctica,

Africa floating not in pale map blue
but the blue of sea, deepest blue,
defining the land in one curved field,
                                        the planet

whole and shining in its black surround.

Naming the New One

They came from mountains and plains
to see the new one, the smooth-skin,
who stood on shaking hind legs
and stared, his eyes struck with light.

"He'll sleep cold," Bear grunted,
and walked away. Bigfoot
was already gone, scared,
and Hummingbird had things to do.

As the others walked and crawled
and flew by, the new one pointed
and hurled a sound at each of them,
louder and louder in his harsh joy.

"Those paws are no good," said Gopher.

"Call him *Wildmouth*," said Deer.
"Does he have ears?"

"He'll learn a song, maybe," said Owl.

Long after the new one stumbled away
they heard him crashing the brush,
still trailing his strange calls.

"Doesn't see where he's going,"
Cougar said.

"Well," said Coyote,
"we'll always know when he's *coming.*"

Coyote acted brave, but he was nervous.
"Let's watch him for a while," he said.
"There's plenty of room. When he finds
his place, then we'll name him."

Toward a New Science Fiction

None of us could explain
the pine that suddenly grew higher
and higher until its limbs
disappeared in blue
and we heard it stretching higher.

We cried out, watching for God
to come down, but nothing appeared
and slowly we calmed.
From all countries we gathered,
pressing hands and cheeks to the bark,
feeling infinity's faint shiver.

The climbers said there were new worlds
to settle, but in a few months
they all came back. The tree
kept going, they told us,
and it wasn't fear that stopped them,

but looking down day after day
as the curving sunlit swirl of Earth
shrank in the dark
until one hand could cover it—
if home wasn't there, they realized,
it wasn't anywhere.

Common Ground

Everywhere on Earth, wet beginnings:

fur, feather, scale, shell, skin, bone, blood,

like an infant discovering sound after sound
a voice is finding itself
in the slop and squall of birth.

It sounds,
and we, in whom Earth happened to light
a clear flame of consciousness,
are only beginning to learn the language—

who are made of the ash of stars,
who carry the sea we were born in,
who spent millions of years learning to breathe,
who shivered in fur at the reptiles' feet,
who trained our hands on the limbs of trees
and came down, slowly straightening
to look over the grasses, to see
that the world not only is
but is beautiful—

we are Earth learning to see itself,
to hear, touch, taste. What it wants to be
no one knows. Finding a way
in starlight and dark, it begins in beauty,

as we begin too, today, tomorrow, now.

Descendants of the Nuclear Age

for David Brower

Whatever they could be
is held in seed—
their faces
containing our faces
in the darkness deeper
than anyone can remember,
their voices
that given speech
will speak for us
when we have passed beyond speech—
whatever it is
the world wants to become
only they can tell,
only in them
can time speak its name
and only in us
can they speak at all,
they speak
if we speak for them.

After the Wedding

for Marilyn

After the white balloons were swept away
on the wind that had swallowed
most of our vows, after the embraces
and tears, the flung rose petals,
after new friends and old friends and aunts
from all over, after you tossed
the bouquet, and the cries of the children
raised coyote cries on the rim,
after chicken grilled on juniper coals,
cold beer from the cattle trough
and hours of hot dancing to Beatles and Stones,
the last of us swaying arms on shoulders,
singing ourselves hoarse,
                    how good it is
to find you now beyond all
the loud joy, driving north in rain
and the lovely ease of our silence.

Ourselves

When the throaty calls of sandhill cranes
echo across the valley, when the rimrock flares
incandescent red, and the junipers
are flames of green on the shortgrass hills,

in that moment of last clear light
when the world seems ready to speak its name,
meet me in the field alongside the pond.
Without careers for once, without things to do,

without dreams or anger or the rattle of fears,
we'll ask how it can be that we walk this ground
and know that we walk, alive in a world
that didn't have to be beautiful, alive

in a world that doesn't have to be.
With no answers, just ourselves and silence,
we'll listen for the song that waits to be learned,
the song that moves through the passing light.

from *All Things Touched by Wind*

1994

Here

If you'll close your eyes and light the inner dark
you'll see a field, a grassy plain extending
to a line of far blue hills, and as you walk
you'll feel the brushing softness of the grass,
its coolness underfoot. You have no memory
of where or why you started, you only know
that the speck you've been approaching rises whole
before you now, a solitary tree
of long and curving limbs, its deep green leaves
shimmering with the breeze that laves your face,
and through the play of leaves you see
the blue of sky, a few bright clouds, the range
of distant hills.

Improbable that a tree
stands here, and you stand too, the steady ground
beneath you, and all around the lively air —
but unlikely as it is, this is exactly
where you've arrived, the place you've never seen
yet recognize, the rendezvous no one arranged.
You can't stay long, you're traveling to the hills
and won't return, so look carefully once more
before you leave. Hills, field, the shimmering tree —
how is it that you're here, to stand and see?

The Meal

The meat is before us, the flagons
have been filled, but my father
doesn't rise to speak. His head
is turned toward the spectacled man
who stares at his plate, and I've seen
that sharp white jaw in a picture —
my grandfather, the lawyer, the one
who died young of syphilis. The candles
glimmer his lenses, he doesn't look up.
Down the table in the crowd of faces
another comes clear, my father's
grandfather, the graybeard harnessmaker
they called Grosspapa, and more
beyond him that I almost know,
their faces obscuring, faint moons
in the dim smoky light. No one
has reached for a fork, the quiet
is awkward now, and I worry
for my father as I used to worry
when the whiskey drugged his tongue.
But he sits straight in his chair,
hands on the edge of the table,
his tie knotted tight. I feel
the familiar weight of his gaze
and a long time passes before
I can look, before I finally see
that the hurt his gray eyes held is gone,
they are clear and burning now,
and helplessly empty of words.
I understand that until I speak
the meal can't begin, all down
the long table they are staring
and waiting, they are hungry, the food
is before them, they have traveled
a great distance to be here.

To My Mother

"I may not live much longer, you know,
and it's all right. I'm thankful
for everything I've had. Do you understand?"

I think I do. I know your eyes shine more
like the sky these days, a stillness
weights your shoulders. I know your swollen feet

and the bones that click in your wrist
when I take your hand can't bear you far.
Soon you are bound from this last house

to the world you love, the world
I love, and I will lose you there,
I will never touch your hand again.

But when tall pines stir with a rising wind,
when the river whispers past my camp,
when breakers sound beyond the brink of dunes,

I will know you by such signs
as I must have known you before I was,
when the anthem of your blood played round

and bathed me in power I breathed and breathed
until at last you could not hold me,
until at last you opened and gave me the world.

In Sky Lakes Wilderness

Winter tells the old stories,
the lakes are shut like eyelids.
Earning heat to pay the wind
we thread our skis between dark firs,
pitch camp as the gray light leaves.
Our fire throws wild shadows
against the circling forest wall,
while beyond that little room
where we drink whiskey, laughing,
the cold stars glint, the wind
touches every tree. Later,
inside our tent, we feel the air
go still, a heaviness, and soon
the ticking of fine snowfall.
As we drift in and out of sleep
we hear the silent storm
begin to bury us, to mound us under
like the bowed young firs.
Our fire hisses faintly as snow
cools and covers it—nothing then
except the creak of limbs
taking on the slow, familiar weight,
and the small whistling flurries
of the wind. Anything we are
makes no difference in this place,
where trees, wind, and falling snow
work their ways together
in the stillness they have always known—
what strange joy, to huddle here
buried in our single warmth,
listening to what lives outside our lives.

Dependence Day

It would be a quieter holiday, no fireworks or loud
parades, no speeches, no salutes to any flag,
a day of staying home instead of crowding away,
a day we celebrate nothing gained in war
but what we're given—how the sun's warmth
is democratic, touching everyone,
and the rain is democratic too,
how the strongest branches in the wind
give themselves as they resist, resist
and give themselves, how birds could have no freedom
without the planet's weight to wing against,
how Earth itself could come to be
only when a whirling cloud of dust
pledged allegiance as a world,
circling dependently around a star, and the star
blossomed into fire from the ash of other stars,
and once, at the dark zero of our time,
a blaze of revolutionary light
exploded out of nowhere, out of nothing,
because nothing needed the light,
as the brilliance of the light itself needs nothing.

To Mt. St. Helens

You were the perfect one,
the saint of symmetry.
We glanced at your benign
bright face, and you shined back
your blessing, you smiled
peacefully upon us.
We didn't much believe
your smoke and stir, we thought
your restiveness would pass—
and then you shuddered hard
and blasted yourself across
four states, engulfed a lake,
gorged rivers with gray mud,
flattened entire forests
and whatever lives they held
in your searing smother.
Your evenness and grace
exploded twelve miles high,
then showered down as grit
on our trim lawns and gardens—
and there you slouch, smudged
and gaping, spewing smoke,
resting in your rubble.
You did it, Mt. St. Helens.
As all of us looked on
you stormed in solitude,
you shrugged and shook aside
what we called beautiful
as if none of us were here,
no animals, no trees,
no life at all outside
your ancient fiery joy—
I admired you, mountain,
but I never loved you until now.

Passages

To listen to the river's muted voice,
its licks and gurgles along the bank,
is to hear the soundless snow
come down in its multitudes
on heights of rock, to hear
that stillness grow dense and deep
in frozen fields, in rivers of ice
grinding bedrock inch by inch—
but quickening then in sheens
and gravelly trickles, joining
in rills down meadowed slopes
pouring themselves into chutes and falls,
pounding down the wooded ravines
with boulder song and rainbow spray,
settling then into rapids
and riffles and swirling pools,
and broadening on in a gliding flow
subdued and lively, deep
with a dreamer's speechful stirring,
lost in this old story that has no end.

The Canyon Wren

for Bruce Bowerman

All afternoon as we hiked up the canyon
with our echoing talk, we heard that bright
long-winded whistle stepping down the scale.
We never saw the bird—only a shadow,
a twitch of limb, as slight and quickly gone

as the lizards flicking across hot stones.
Where the streambed steepened to dry waterfall
we almost quit, our packs absurdly heavy,
the rocks we jarred loose clattering below,
that sky-filled notch of canyon drawing us on.

We camped by a few scummed pools, loud with frogs,
and climbing on in the morning we didn't find
the big surprise we'd hoped for: no bighorn sheep,
no petroglyphs, no monster waterfall,
just more and more of tumbled boulders, clumps

of prickly pear, dry sand with fool's gold glint,
the same heat shimmer in the same still air,
and once in a while, from somewhere close, the wren's
clear song. And then, that evening, something more.
We walked into the canyon's trick of quiet,

into the ease of being just where we were,
the great walls shouldering high, flooded with moon,
and down the gorge, Death Valley in pale haze.
As we sat late by crumbling coals, the wind
came glancing, grazing our faces, alive

in the limbs of the junipers, dying down now
and rising, returning its song. Across
cool stones, along the canyon's shadowed curves,
through all the secret slickrock passages
the wind came softly, and its voice spoke for our own.

Opal Creek

A narrow, twisting trail enters this woods
of hemlock, red cedar, and Douglas fir,
follows the stream flashing white through trees,
switchbacks across steep ridges, and grows fainter
as the tilted, mossy-barked trees grow huger
and fallen trunks lie everywhere, roots upthrust,
their solid centuries drawn back to ground,
ranks of seedlings rooted in the rotting wood.

Grow and go down, the dark earth spiring to light
and returning, the forest travels its changing way
without the need of any trail to guide it,
and neither do the varied thrush and winter wren
need direction through the shadows where they sing,
or the red-backed vole that burrows in the ground,
or the stream spuming and swirling between pools.
Only we humans who walk here need this line

that leads through stillness and muted light,
through ferns and thimbleberry sopping our pants,
through the blended dark smells of mossy ground,
through scatters of mushrooms yellow and crimson
and flaring orange, others half-black half-white—
and even we can stray, even women and men
can gradually learn to let go of the trail
as it fades among trees and underbrush

and leaves us where nothing human shows the way.
There are other ways. We can lower ourselves
on vine maple holds down a moss-slick bank,
thrash through a tangle of devil's club and briars,
climb from the thicket on a down Douglas fir
and walk that trunk to another, and another,
and at last to one great fallen tree, thicker through
than we are tall. We can climb its furrowed bark

and sit for a while, our hard breath easing,
as we listen to a bird hidden high above.
Like the spiring trees and the lives they hold,
we rest ourselves on death's generous body,
and all around us where the stillness sings
we see the green abundance of death's rising.
We came for this, to join for an afternoon
the long dance of the trees, and when we turn

to find the trail and walk out of the forest,
we take with us what surrounds us in this place
by leaving it here, where it belongs—
where mushrooms, moss, and red-backed vole,
where thimbleberry and dripping ferns,
where thrush and wren and the unseen birds,
where swirling stream and muted light,
where stillness and the ancient trees go on.

The Kid Who Asked Too Many Questions

for Nathan Hamilton

All our walk long the boy had wondered
why some rocks were big and some
not so big, why this tree died
and that one lived, why juniper berries
were the blue of sky—so bye and bye
I grumbled up a thunderstorm
and lightning split him eye for eye.
His halves settled, two gray stones
stuck in the ground with no voice
to ask, "What happened?" Between them,
where all that wanting to know
had seethed behind the boy's eyes,
the yellow balsamroot blooms in May,
and lizards wait for a question
to the answer beneath their feet.

The European Birch

for Denise Levertov

Half the world from the birthplace
of its kind, its white
trunk scarred
and flecked with moss,
wet and gleaming,
its branches fountaining
into leafless twigs—where
but in this rain
does the birch belong?
It gathers
the falling formlessness
so that each twig-tip
and joint of twig
bears one clear drop,
one cosmos
glowing from within,
each held in wholeness
by the sheer
tension of its forming,
and the drops all together
this autumn afternoon
compose the tree
in its distinction, standing clear.

The Echoing Lake

for John Stacey

Cadence of our hissing skis, soft crunch of poles,
across the lake's clear calm we push and glide,
the fresh snow glittering with sparks of moon,
and circling round as if for ceremony,
the black upthrusted points of silent trees.

We slogged in miles for this, to solve our lives
for just an evening by this algebra
of light and dark, and the world will never stand
in stricter clarity—yet how we fit
in its cold beauty isn't clear. The moon's

blank face says nothing, and around it flares
a text of glinting hieroglyphic fire
our minds can't comprehend, inscrutable
as our own shadows skiing next to us,
and the sharply spiring silhouettes of trees.

But listen—when we stop and sing the tones
just right, those dark hemlocks and Douglas firs
enclose us in the chord of our own voices,
hovering like our breath-clouds in the air,
shimmering with the flashing snow and stars.

In Thanks for Feeling Happier

The wind that wakes the aspen leaves
rises from its absence into song—
spirit remembers, stirs itself,
sings now without intent to sing,
aimlessly and exactly sure,
a shimmering in sunlit air.

To the Scrub Jay on my Office Mate's Desk

As if you know what you're doing
you flick through the window
and here you are, brighter blue
than I've ever seen you in sun,
at ease and cocking your head
as if born for the company
of Kent's papers and cups.
I'll be late for class, stout-bill,
but I have to know why you flew in
to this fluorescent cave
from the air of a fine spring day,
and what's on your mind
as you hop past the stapler —

— and how I can keep you
from the half-open door
just a wing-lift away.
Don't do it, bird.
I can just see you
lost in the halls, slapping
the ceiling tiles, glancing
off dim painted walls,
careening into my class
with your croaking panic
and dodging the startled faces,
flapping and clawing, grazing
the blackboard, finally thrashing
your chalk-smeared feathers
against the window, crazy
for the blue afternoon . . .
That might arouse their interest.

But you have better sense.
With a flex of your legs,
a brush of air on my cheek,
you leave as you came. You're
out where you should be.
I'm left with the half-open door.

The Gray Whales Passing Point Reyes

With geysering spouts the whales break into sun and plunge
        steady southward, flukes tossed high
and sliding under sea. All afternoon they pass, three and four
        at a time, still weeks away

from the Baja lagoons where they'll breach and frolic
        and birth their young,
six thousand miles from the Arctic ice to lounge a few weeks
        in those warm seas—

those seas where Scammon's men a century ago speared calves
        to get the mothers, spouts
shooting blood, flukes thrashing the water to crimson froth,
        and the salt flats stinking of peeled bones

as the northern prairies stank of bison shot from trains,
        stripped of tongue and three-dollar hide . . .
that square-shouldered pleasure bringing big things down.
        We aim binoculars now, shoot

only pictures, crowding the lighthouse rail and exclaiming
        as a new spout rises,
a glistening back breaks water and plunges away.
        Steadily, easily

they move with the urge that drives them, huge bodies small
        in the spangled sea
and small in the scope of their great journey, traveling
        this trail of rough-rocked coast

that in March they'll follow north again, the new calves
       swimming alongside their mothers
to the Bering Sea's blue cold. We watch and keep watching
       as if hypnotized, not by the creatures

we see only for seconds but by the long unfaltering line
       of their passage, on and on
through the afternoon and steadily into the twilit haze,
       as we drift from the rail

and blend in the highway's flow—bright stream that bears us
       to the dinners and sleeps
of our singular lives, and each of us on to new places and homes,
       to travels and travels

but no journey together like the journey of the whales,
       no path that might gather us
and lead us around through the turning of seasons and back
       to ourselves, again and again,

looping our one life through the lengths of Earth's time.

First Things First

Dreaming, when I ask Wendell Berry
for seeds, his hands turn the leaves
of a bulky loose book, bulging
with woven and waxpaper pouches—
specks, fat kernels, wings and barbs,
corn and ricegrass tucked under straps,
tufts of wheat and long-eared oats
on the pages his hands keep turning.
"What kind did you want?" he says.
I forgot as the pages went by.
"Where do you live?" he's asking now,
and I know, of course, or thought I did . . .
"Well, take what you want," he says,
with a grin. "But don't you think
you'll need a place to plant 'em?"

A *Prayer among Friends*

Among other wonders of our lives, we are alive
with one another, we walk here
in the light of this unlikely world
that isn't ours for long.
May we spend generously
the time we are given.
May we enact our responsibilities
as thoroughly as we enjoy
our pleasures. May we see with clarity,
may we seek a vision
that serves all beings, may we honor
the mystery surpassing our sight,
and may we hold in our hands
the gift of good work
and bear it forth whole, as we
were borne forth by a power we praise
to this one Earth, this homeland of all we love.

The Pelicans of San Felipe

do most of their fishing asleep on the sand,
great bills lowered to their breasts.
Overhead the gulls cry *now*, and *now*,
but the pelicans drowse in the plenty of time.
The sand is warm, the breeze enfolds them,
the steady waves rumble and slosh.
Two or three together through the afternoon,
they raise their monkish white heads
and lift from the beach, mute as in sleep,
winging their way above the green swells
to join the others now circling low,
and circling low, and each in its moment
with a quick tilt of wings falls hard,
gracelessly smacks the sea—
then bobbing up quickly, riding the swells,
wild gulls veering and screaming around them,
the pelicans lift their bills and swallow.

Unbound

for W. S. Di Piero

Squares of tended grass, roses
trimmed and mulched with chips,
all the blank front doors along
these gridded streets, this
neighborhood I walk and carry
docilely in mind—until
one yellow leaf shoots by
and I'm on edge again, I'm
walking fast through gusting air
that strips the maples, scattering
leaves and paper scraps
like some rousing consciousness
unbound by human blocks—as if
the wild god had wakened me,
or waked in me, not the clerk
who accounts for fallen birds,
the one we kicked upstairs,
but the god still ranging
in this world, that scatters us
to its unspoken need, and only
finds its way as we find ours.

The Unseen

1

Mustard crowds the barbed-wire fence,
the entire hillside thick with light
and glowing brighter as the pale sky
goes dim. The single oak is hazed
with April leaves. Across the valley
children call, quick strokes of sound.
A wavering cloud of sparrows passes,
a kestrel hovers on beating wings —
impossibly much, but I need more tonight
than the bare glory of what's given.
I need to rub this moment in mind
for the shimmer of meaning I almost see,
I need the boy who stood shivering once
in a different field, hands clenched
at his sides in the clammy dusk
as he silently burned into mind
the whippoorwills, silhouettes of trees,
the bright clear blue of the west —
I'll remember, he whispered, *even
when I'm dead I'll remember this.*

2

It always came to emptiness,
a dark wind,
the light of cold stars
passing through me—
I breathed once,
I walked in my body.
Nothing, I don't know,
I'd say when my mother asked
what made me cry,
and as the light went out—
switch on, switch off—I knew
that even the dream was wrong,
that when I died
there would be no stars,
nothing in my mind,
no *me,*
and I would not return in all of time.

3

Birdsong woke me to the hunger.
As pale light filled the window
I watched with one eye open,
wondering what I wanted —
nothing in my parents' house
or school or Sunday school
but something I had never tasted,
something in the still trees,
the songs of hidden birds
calling in the cool morning
as I still slept, it was nowhere
in the world and everywhere,
if I could just find words to name it.

4

I lay on the pavement trying to see.
The snake raised
his broken neck, swaying,
as if there was something
he still needed.
I was looking for the moment.
His jaws stretched, and from deep
in the darkness of his throat
a dry hiss forced its way.
In a spasm, he subsided.
It was the spirit leaving him,
I told myself, pressing
the skin of his small piled body.
He twitched and lay still.
I heard the spirit,
I said out loud, and stood
in the stillness of the summer afternoon.

5

I'd sit where the trunk divided and watch
how the limbs
divided again,
how the branches branched
and made themselves
a confusion of a million
twig-ends touching air.
And I wondered—
if a bud on one twig-end
awakened
by itself,
if all it saw
was twigs and buds and sky,
could it ever know
where it came from?
How, before it opened
as a leaf and fell,
how could it think its way
back through
those chance divisions,
through the entire
blind branching history
that had brought it to its place in empty air?

6

Kneeling by the animal tracks I didn't know,
I felt hidden eyes
upon me, close, and everything
stood clearer, brighter then,
each twig, each fallen leaf
in the puddles from the morning's rain.
As I hiked back through woods and fields
where nothing moved but me,
watched by something wild
that stirred my groin and made me whip around
to stare at only stones and honeysuckle,
the hillside's green horizon,
the shining of last light on boughs—
those things meant more
than just themselves, they stood
for everything I couldn't know
but was close around me
as I walked home,
hollow-bellied with happiness,
beneath the darkening forest trees
and the bright scattered tracks of all the stars.

7

Wind on the waters, rippling there,
rippling the reeds
that gracefully give way
and rest.
        Now
downshore the rippling reeds,
now here again,
as the water quickens
with sheens and glints.
If it were given I would come back.
If it were given
I would roam here always,
touching the face of what I loved.

8

Fired with sun, the red-tail drifts
deep in the sky, circling
higher and higher
in that volume of light,
and drowsing below
I dream and drift along,
I feel the streaming air,
the land turning beneath me—
to die might feel like this,
my speck of self ascending
so far into the light
that it becomes the light at last.
And now as I rise to go, I see
near my imprint in the grass
two yellow slugs,
curled in semicircles
and stroking each other
with their snouts,
stretching filaments of slime
as they stroke. They raise
their blind, faceless mouths,
they stir themselves in the light of sun.

9

This is the path where the panther waits,
shadowing the things of day.
His keen eyes glow. I call them stars.
His breath stirs. I call it wind.
His black coat quickens, and this
is the place I always falter,
this is the shadow
of his unborn leap,
where he waits to rend
my hide of fear,
where I might be born,
or disappear.

10

Paralyzed, I see
my heart gone still.
My hands can't reach
to squeeze it, pound it
to life again. Arteries
around it stiffen.
I give up then.
And from those roots
and the cold stone
they circumscribe,
a great tree grows—
I watch it rise,
watch it swaying
in the light of sky,
and I feel my body
stretch and tremble.

11

High to the north a snow peak stands in the last
deep light,
the nameless one
that sends this black-water stream
swirling through the chill of dusk.
Nothing
in the stream's quick passing,
nothing in the snow
and silent trees,
nothing in the mountain glowing with last sun,
nothing here knows
my presence,
nothing will be lesser
when I've gone.
It isn't much,
this shivering warmth
I cradle like a candle,
worried how it flickers,
how it burns low—
I would let it burn,
I would turn it loose
to the beautiful indifference of this world,
where the first stars
are shining,
the mountain stands in stillness,
and the stream swirls
past one small light in the darkening trees.

12

If the way is anywhere, it's here
in the dodge and mingle of mustard flowers
flattening as the wind comes on,
in the blue eucalyptus swirling wild
with a shimmer of water-sound,
and even in the stiff oak limbs
that stir as if remembering just now
what motion is. It doesn't seem
so difficult, this fluid aimlessness,
this ease with which things bend
as they hold firm—what flows in trees
and ripples silvery through the grass
is loosening my fearbound spirit,
that thinking tried and tried to free.
If I can learn this limbering,
if I can dance this Earthly dance
like all things touched by wind,
when the hour comes I might be ready
to swirl loose from all I know.

New and Uncollected Poems

1994 - 2010

Working Draft

Still half in my dream I see the memoir I'm writing,
the familiar manuscript pages,
and a sure and stately voice
is speaking the prose
just as it should be spoken,
as I never can—
but the words, the words themselves
elude me, now that I listen,
the voice is a river of syllables not quite said,
and the type
though it is my font
won't focus either,
nor the penned-in edits,
as if I were trying to read under water—
this isn't my memoir,
it's a text I've forgotten,
my best book maybe,
already in draft,
and now as it's time to leave I'm frantic to have it,
but the pages hover
just out of reach as I rise away,
the sure voice fading,
and now as my eyes are about to open
I see—
I didn't make this manuscript,
the manuscript is making *me*,
the life inside my life,
composing, revising, imagining on,
down in the depths whose lit surface I just now break.

Spring Burning

One April morning in the rain I pile green boughs
from the big Douglas fir
whose limbs had sagged on the barn.
I splash gas, toss a match, and *whump*
out of nowhere, an orange explosion
subsiding to a hesitant burn,
flames stirring like sleepy children
still thralled by the other world.
Then a quickening hiss and crackle
of sap-gorged wood, and the flames
remember their yellow hunger,
climbing the heaped greens with a rising roar.
I heave more branches,
my hat lowered to the sheer smack of heat
that instantly sizzles the needle-sprays black,
singes my mustache, frizzes
the hairs on the backs of my hands,
and I wonder as I feed it
big sections of limb
how we ever got it locked in the tips of matches
or in motors idling at our feet,
how we trained it to simmer saucepans
or stand, docile, on candle wicks,
a flutter as one of us walks by
the one slight sign
that once the world was its seething cauldron
and is that yet, within.
Live, I say, tossing junk wood now,
rotted shingles and posts,
a wobbly sawhorse —
Live now, and not this summer.
But it isn't for prudence or precaution
that I feed and feed
that unbearable aura,

it's for the flames that exult around each gift,
transforming hard heft
in their red livid heart
to the nothing it was and is.
Ashes drift down with the sprinkling rain.
With no more to offer
I stand aside, gazing like a kid
at the great burning tent I will someday enter—
it gathers itself
from the dull clay ground,
it writhes and yearns, it points
to the far, invisible stars it has not forgotten.

A Candle in Solitude

February 14, 2001

On the table in the pewter stick
you sent with me, it throws light
to write this by, my supper done,
rain soft-drumming the cabin roof.
I watch the flame standing
not quite still on its melted pool.
A bluish dark hovers within it,
around the curved black wick
whose tip glows red, the pale
body of the greater flame
pouring upward into shadow,
wavering like a thing alive—
like nothing but itself, but still,
it reminds me of those does
this morning, how their ears
twitched and slightly turned,
and the little screech owl
a few nights ago, bobbing
and tilting in my flashlight beam.

The flame's been upright,
holding quiet for minutes,
but now with a draft that I can't feel
it leans, quivering, and I see you—
an inclination of your face
that I know well, and that lively
stillness when you sleep, rapt
within a dream . . .

The candle flickers—
did I speak? I heard your laugh,
I thought, your purest laugh,
as if something I'd just said
delighted you, as if the flame
were your conscious mind itself,
hearkening across the table—
and now *I* laugh, remembering
that I'm the one who all this time's
been hearkening to it, my love, to you.

A Mind of Winter

All day the snow's been gusting slant and swirling
in the pasture, snow of the sky,
fallen snow up-aired again,
trees and distance lost
in the whirling white,
the stovepipe whistling, groaning, as the wind
rushes and turns on itself
and buffets the barn's tin roof.
I wouldn't last long out there,
but creatures in their burrows do,
and now, as the wind
slackens, maybe they hear the fine tremble
of snow touching down,
maybe their minds gather a glowing white warmth.
Will I ever remember
why I was born?
If I knew, it left me in the wild wind
that now eases to rumors beneath the eaves
and then goes quiet.
As snow still falls, sparsely,
the thinning storm-murk swells
with soft radiance
as if lit from within.
If anything can know what I want to know,
this luminous moment
might be its mind.
The pines and junipers stand, their boughs filled,
as fine crystals drift down
in changing light, spirited entirely by what they are.

Blue Heron in the Cloverleaf

Brake lights flash as we take
the onramp curve—
has your plumed head gone daft?
Why pick *here* to stand
on your backward knees?
No fish, no frogs
on this grass plot,
just an eddy of fumes
that we keep fresh and swirling.
Your s-curved neck
tucks forward
as you step—
an Eldorado squeals,
nearly rams a Nova,
and you
stop still as death.
We've got you hypnotized,
and your blue dignity
has us fouled up.
Our sleek craft arc
erratically around your earth
until our progress
feeds us to the freeway,
where what else can we do
but look ahead and hit the gas.

Blowout

Deepwater Horizon, Spring 2010

Few of us have seen the stuff itself,
the remains of epochs, eras,
of algae and protozoans
long buried beneath layers of rock.
Few have seen or touched it,
but the toddler absorbs a trace
when she mouths the plastic toy,
as do all of us who eat from fields
fertilized and sanitized
with its efficient derivatives.

We get whiffs of it from traffic,
from the weed-whacker and mower,
and sometimes a raw breath comes
as we board a plane, then again
disembarking in a distant city,
a trail of white streaks lingering
behind, dissolving slowly
in the hazy skies of a warming day.

We know it by such hints and spoor,
but so carefully have we trained it
to do its work for us and keep
discreetly out of sight and mind
that we don't know crude oil—
this brown or greenish or coal-black goo
that clogs with crippling weight
the pelican's wings, floods beach
and marshland in a dark tide
that does not ebb.

Those good souls
who net the birds and clean them,
who blot the shorelines as they can
with paper pads, they know its feel,
its balled or caked or oozing heft,
and they know in nose and throat
its sulfurous stink. But they, at least,
can shed their gloves and boots
and sleep clean tonight—or would
sleep clean, if any of us could.

Remember that man in the movies?
The wildcatter, drilling for his dream,
strikes it big and dances now
in the black rain of his spewing well,
smeared, soaked, besotted with oil,
screaming his triumph, his face
so writhed he seems almost in agony.
He has it all, this oiled man.
He is rich now, he's crazy rich,
but he means to share his dream.
He sees great things for all of us.
His gusher has come in and it is ours.

A Speculation on the First and Second Tools

Maybe the men's faces glowed in firelight
as one struck stone to stone,
then stared at the glassy flake
that he'd knapped free—
and cut his finger feeling its edge,
then grabbed a hunk
of stiffened hide and sliced it clean.
Did they shout then?
Stand and slash at air with what he'd made?

The women may have stilled their hands
and glanced, curious,
amused perhaps,
then turned again to cleaning roots,
to sorting berries
or threshing seed—
for the children, for themselves,
and for the exulting men,
food they had gathered
leaning to the ground
each with two free hands,
babies riding their sides in woven slings.

Stretching Out on a Picnic Table off U.S. 101

Wind in the redwoods, sunlit branches
      swirling deep

in the blue of sky, fire-scarred trunks
      swaying, the heartwood

stretching, two thousand years awake
      in the wind. A car

whines then fades in the anthem of boughs,
      wind in my hair,

shadow and sunlight alive on my face
      and deep inside

as I rise high into the trees to sleep.

To a Reed College Sophomore Soon to Drop Out, Fall 1967

Well, it's clear you're not the talking kind,
but I can see you, at least—you're cadging
steak-night scraps in Commons, learning to climb
on Gorge basalt, writing a paper for Hum 110
all night in Eliot Hall, and grilling burgers

in the coffee shop amid laughter not yours.
Why do you cling so hard to loneliness?
Why fear what you most want—to open up?
Trust more. That's mainly what I've got to say.
But you're not answering, so I'll go on.

Be more skeptical of drugs, more respectful
of the classes and professors you consider
irrelevant to your life. You don't *have*
a life, remember? You drift the campus—
drizzling fall, flowering spring—hoping life

will track you down and jump you in a flash
of knowing. You yearn for enlightenment.
I've got good news for you on that, but first,
the bad. You'll never find it. Not in acid,
your desultory Zen, or anything else—

not in your first sixty years, anyway.
I write, you see, and if I were enlightened,
surely I'd be selling a lot more books.
Yes, I'm a writer, as you hope to be,
though you hope with scant belief. I have

a home, too, a wife, stepsons, grandkids even.
I've got a life. And I'd like to know, of course,
how you would rate it. But you're stone quiet,
you deaf-mute boy, and just as well. The man
you have become might disappoint you.

I prefer martinis to pot or mescaline.
I buy from businesses you would despise.
The U.S. is waging needless war again—
I hate it, but I don't resist. I don't
give rides to hitchhikers. I own things

and tread in rutted habits you would scorn,
you with your pure, prideful intolerance.
I'm compromised. But look, you should be pleased
that I'm still here—and that I've learned,
in our forty-five years apart, the good news

about enlightenment. You don't need it.
Follow the truest hungers of your spirit,
and the common light of day will do you fine.
One thing will lead to another, and through
the good and painful years you'll realize

that life is not still hazily ahead
or off in a distant land, but here, now, you.
You'll do not as well as your best hopes
but far better than your worst fears, and this
you will call happiness. Trust me on it.

Poem for Fern Ridge Library

Read then, if you will,
and in the springtime of your reading
the pages will shine with pale fire,
like new alder leaves in sun.
In their secret way they grow
and gather as you turn them,
they remain with you, they rise up
close around like blackberry thickets
in midsummer, a wilderness
of leaves you're lost in. Turn,
turn further. Something shy
and never seen awaits you,
and as you search you may discover
what you did not think to ask for,
a last apple in autumn boughs
where you saw a bird fly in.
Listen. In the Douglas firs the wind
is saying something, voice
of distant places, other years returning.
Does it speak your name?
You need nothing more for winter now,
the faithful rain on your roof,
a warm fire within. Go
the way you were born to go,
turning and turning the pages of time.

If, Like Me, You Are Not an Oregon Native but Wish You Were

1
Roll your eyes, laugh loud,
derisively,
throw a punch even,
when someone calls it
"ARE—uh—gahn."

2
Call a downpour "a little rain."
Call rain "mist."
Call mist "sunlight."
Call sunlight "too damn much like California for me."

3
Study journals of the Oregon Trail.
Buy an antique pen, some ink,
and a sheaf of hemp paper.
Write a journal of the Oregon Trail,
rich with misery and fortitude,
by your great-grandfather.
Bind the journal in rawhide.
Spill coffee and stew on the pages.
Age it for years half-buried
in the high desert, discover it
in your attic and call the local news.

4
In September, make sure
you say *filbert*,
even though it rhymes
with "Dilbert"
and your inner voice
keeps screaming,
HAZELNUT!

5

In the country, resist the urge
to hug trees. In the woods
with others, nod your head
and say, "Nice timber there."
Buy a chainsaw, keep it sharp,
and know how to use it.
It's a flat dead giveaway
to drop a tree on yourself.

6

If you're serious about this,
have a child in Oregon
and name it after you.
Send the kid to live
with grandparents in Maine,
or, even better, with a nice
Siberian family,
and steal the kid's identity.
(Ask the kid how to do this
on the family computer
before shipping him or her away.)

7

If nothing else works, try this.
Die in the rain and dissolve
in a puddle. Get reborn
as a slug and work your way
toward the human again.
Haunt each body you inhabit
with one indelible thought:
"I don't know why, but I must
return to the puddle to die."
Be patient. When finally
you are born as a human being,

pray that the first mouth
to kiss you will be berry-stained
and fragrant with salmon,
and if the first words to form
in your mouth are, "No sales tax,
damn it!"—you are born again,
this time in the best of states.

The River

September 11, 2001

From its source in the first, farthest cordilleras of time,
the river surges with stars
exploding into gas and dust
that flow on into new stars and planets.
It streams, radiant, from the sun,
through the thousands
of millions of years
and innumerous lives
of our Earth. It sweeps and moans
in the blasting currents
of snowstorms high in the mountains,
where the river in time
reawakens as water,
and tonight, as I step out into starlit quiet,
its subdued chant rises
from deep in the canyon,
whispering the story of its own being.
We belong to that story,
but the river can't say
why today some die while others live on,
or why it should be
that we die at all,
or why we should live.
To the river we mean no more or less
than the miners
who sluiced their gold
from its crannies
and hunted and killed the Indians
and drove them away,
and the Indians,
their fire smoke rising for thousands of years
to a glittering heaven,

meant no more or less to the river
than all other lives
that have known its green
and rushing white waters.
Again and again the river has thundered
with killing floods,
run thick with torrents of volcanic ash,
dwindled in drought
to a rank trickle
and freshened again,
bountiful with death and life.
The river does not ask and does not choose.
It rises, it gathers
all that it touches and goes its way.
In surging falls and deep green pools, in chutes
and riffles and silent swirls,
it bears us on through winding reaches
of grace and fury,
until once, perhaps,
in a stab of sun on streaming water
the entire aching beauty of being comes clear.
And the river—the good, green, terrible river—flows on.

The Wind in Sand Creek Canyon

T. H. Watkins
1936 – 2000

A small wind in Sand Creek Canyon touches bootprints,
figures inscribed in stone,
it sifts through sage and rabbitbrush,
lifts cottonwood leaves
and lays them down.

No, the wind in Sand Creek Canyon stirs
as it often stirs, stirs
already where it will be
when this line finds its end.
And the wind itself will end,
and the great cliffs too,
this blind, beautiful carving of time
that receives our love so silently.
We love it all the more,
you and I said once, for knowing
that it must vanish and we
much sooner, blessed to have lived our instant
in the time of stone,
the time of sky,
our faces fresh to the wind.

I began to tell you, Tom,
that the wind stirs dust
and glances up side canyons
looking for you in a place you loved—but you,
good editor, remind me
that the wind won't bear that weight.
The wind contains no sorrow,
no searching need, as you
bear no more sorrow and no more need.

You are the wind, dear friend,
and now, before this line
finds its end, the wind in Sand Creek Canyon has moved on.

Christmas Psalm in Solitude

Spirit whose name I do not know,
Spirit of darkened meadow and the pointed trees
    silhouetted around me,
Spirit of the great sky strewn with stars,
Spirit of streamwater swirling over mossy stones
    down to the old and ageless river,
Spirit of salmon and steelhead facing the current,
    holding in darkened pools,
Spirit of bears adrift in their rank havens
    and veering bats sounding the night,
Spirit of moles and earthworms and the smaller lives
    thriving underground,

Spirit whose name I do not know,
Spirit of vole and plunging owl,
Spirit of doe with fawn in her belly, Spirit
    of cougar who rips the belly,
Spirit of the garden and the snake in the garden,
Spirit of chance and purpose, of all that has been
    and all that shall be,
Spirit of the one way and Spirit of the many,
Spirit of all ends and beginnings,

Spirit whose name I do not know,
Though it glints in fire across the sky tonight
    and speaks itself in silence,
Though as near as this clay ground I stand on,
Though I hear it in the stream singing in darkness
    and the river whispering below,
Though it is part of me like the breath that clouds
    and vanishes before me,
Spirit within me, Spirit without, Spirit of form
    and the absence of form,
Spirit of these mountains rising and wearing away,

Spirit whose name I do not know,
Of all who sleep or wake in these mountains tonight
I am the one who doubts and falters, who loses
    himself in distraction,
I am the one who sees and smells and hears the least
    and stumbles the most,
But I am the one who speaks words aloud
    with mouth and tongue,
And tonight I speak to praise you, Spirit,
Because in all that I name and cannot name
I know you are born, you are born this night
    and all nights and all days,
And you are here in these mountains, in this river canyon,
    and in all places of Earth.

Spirit whose name I do not know,
Though tonight or tomorrow or a day sure to come
    I must fall to the clay,
To the stones and flowing cold waters,
Though my body must burn to ash or dry into dust
    or molder, tunneled by worms,
Though I must relinquish this small light of mind
    I have thought of as my own,
Though I know these things as surely as I now breathe,
Though I stand afraid tonight in this meadow,
Spirit, I understand tonight and I accept tonight
    that in this darkness lives your way.

Spirit whose name I do not know,
Beneath your fierce stars and the black of space
I rejoice tonight that you are born,
And that Earth and its numberless lives are born of you,
And the other worlds and their numberless lives,

And I rejoice tonight that in all creatures born,
    bacterium to blue whale,
You yourself are born, you honor us to bear your desire
    to be flesh and bone and blood,
To be the suffering of illness and dying,
To be the pleasures and agonies of love,
To be the joys of consciousness and also its griefs.

Spirit whose name I do not know,
Though I am afraid tonight, and tremble tonight,
I am glad beyond measure that in finding your way
    you have given me life,
And I am glad beyond measure that in finding my way
    I in some small manner give life to you.
I thank you this night for the privilege of being.
I thank you this night for the mind and heart and voice
    with which I now speak.
I thank you this night for my life, my death, and all
    lives and deaths that may come of me.
Though I will not know who I am, I shall serve you
    and serve your journey forevermore,
On Earth and in all the darkness and fire of the heavens.

Morning Song, Winter Creek

White remnants in the tall firs—
it *did* snow,
I didn't dream it.
But I did—
you and I weightless,
two shy spirits
twining
high in the trees
where we've never been,
each bough
delicately
holding snow
on soft green needles,
in moonlight
warm and cool
on our skin
like a slight summer wind.

I think we wanted to know
what the trees know,
to gather
and bear lightly
what comes—
storm, warm breeze,
and somehow,
my love,
the two of us too,
spiriting together
among those boughs,
as light and alive as moonlight itself.

The Ancient Bristlecone Pine Forest

Here on their mountaintop it's all rock,
sun, and stubby trees,
the trunks twisted
inside out, more
bare grain than bark,
as if the oldest trees on Earth
were writhing to leave it.
The ripping storms
of four thousand winters
have cropped their limbs
to broken brushes
of blunt needles.
Yet somehow
what they need
is here, surrounded
in sky, where scree
drifts downslope
faster than trees can grow.
Open brown cones
gather around the trunks—
roots clenched in stone
answer wind, snow, centuries
with that same steady speech.

To a Friend Who Doubts
That Her Writing Matters

Yes, the evening light was lovely and full
before the thrush fluted
its up-spiraling song,
but if the thrush had held its voice,
I wouldn't have looked
just now, wouldn't
have seen this mossy oak limb golden in sun
and felt a pang of joy.
I didn't see the thrush.
I don't know why it sang.
Because it is a thrush, I guess,
and because it is the thrush it is
and would stir the silence in its own way.
Sing for no one, Emma,
and sing for us all, sing
for the one you may never know
who will waken, somewhere, to your voice.

For a Wedding under Mount Adams

In places on the mountain we don't know,
ice releases shinings over stone
that teach themselves to trickle, splash,
and sing in tongues, to smooth the edges
of sharp rocks and marry them to moss.
This flowing song goes quiet in grasses,
unfolds in fronds of fern, and rises
year by year in stands of alder and fir.
Through boughs and shrubs and wildflowers
Earth exchanges vows with sun,
and the wedding party comes from far.
Old travelers surge up chutes and rapids
to hover in pools, betrothed to death
and to the lives they bear. In their journey,
in the great tides of snow and rain,
a distant sea returns the mountain's call,
and such company answers your love too.
You marry more than you or any can tell—
you marry all that's here, and marry well.

A Word with William Stafford

> You can't tell when strange things with meaning
> will happen. I'm [still] here writing it down
> just the way it was.
>
> —*William Stafford, handwritten unsteadily*
> *the morning of August 28, 1993, the day he died.*

Bill Stafford, you shifty old stalwart,
you never would tell me if my poems
were good. Yes, you vouched for me
when I wanted work or a fellowship,
and I'm pretty sure your word helped.
I did wonder, though—was it my poetry

you liked, or only my good intentions,
my sincere but unseasoned striving?
It would be years before I understood
the generosity in your silence.
A poet writes poems, you didn't say,
his best might be born tomorrow,

and praise for what's already written
serves that birth no better than scorn.
Stay alert, you said. Be ready. Practice
the little ways that invite good fortune.
Old maker, thank you for your answer,
and here is my confession and pledge:

I still believe less in what I have written
than in what I hope still to write.
And so, like you, I will follow this pen
right into that day when my scrawl skips
and stutters like a shaky seismograph
and skids out of language off the page.

The Canyon

Here below as the sun slides past its zenith
in the pale October sky, below
the crumbling basalt of the canyon rim
that spewed in fire when it was young,
now water-stained and streaked with lichen,
below the deeper layers of sand and chalk
containing lives that flourished once
when a warm sea lapped and pounded here,
below the bright crowns of ponderosa pines
and homely junipers, finding our way
on the canyon floor among silvered snags,
alongside the stream with its quiet song
discovering deeper and deeper ages—here
we walk and rest with our good years together,
plucking juniper berries, sprigs of sage,
crushing them to breathe their savor,
to stain ourselves with this place we love,
this place where time allows us to roam
as if all time were ours, as if our hearts
beat to the rhythm of volcanic storms
and we breathed to rising and falling seas,
as if—as if, even as we idle here,
time itself were not scouring this gorge
of every trace of our two lives, as if
even now, slowly—not slowly at all—
time were not drowning us, each from the other,
from ourselves and all our places.
                                        My love,
there is no snag or tree that we can cling to,
no ledge where we might climb from the flood
to watch our own spent bodies wash away—
and yet, I tell you, because it is true,
we are the luckiest of all time's fools
to be alive together, exactly here,
so lost in where we are and will not be

that we wander wholly, helplessly free,
following the canyon at our own pace
as it shows us down, with water song
and the odor of sage, through the long
unfolding of the late afternoon,
our faces glowing with the same cool warmth
that lights the pines and junipers,
that brightens the bedrock of an ancient sea
and fires far above us the rimrock cliffs,
cracked and stained, crusted with age,
all flaws revealed to the deepening light—
faces, my love, such as we too must wear,
faces like those we wear today, beautiful
for all time brings and all it bears away.

The Barn

Wind clatters the loose tin roof of the barn today
as it did thirty-five years ago,
when I lived here
and wrote that sound
into what I hoped was a poem.
Sweet hay filled the barn back then,
children filled a pail with warm squirts
and left the milk cow safe for the night.
I've forgotten the cow's name now,
the kids and bales are gone
and the barn itself is going,
board after board splayed loose by sun and storm.
The door swings on squalling hinges.
Snow blows in through the gaping walls
and swirls on the packed earth floor,
where a coffee can and scraps of wire,
withered corpses of mice,
and splinters of the barn's own body
lie where they have lain for years.
It was made, they say, down-valley somewhere
before anyone can remember,
dismantled and rebuilt here
close to the year I was born.
And now that sparse history too is falling away
with its warped boards
and tattered roof, and I say good.
Why should the barn hold on to what it cannot keep?
Let it strip down now to its surest self,
to the stalwart posts and beams
that nameless makers long in the ground
adzed and joined with pegs.
Let the frame stand as long as it will,
let hawks perch there by day
and owls by night,

let the spirited air that once pummeled the walls
now whistle freely through,
let it burnish those timbers smooth
of history and time itself, of everything
but the old keen light of the Hunter's moon
as it arcs long and mute across the clear cold night.

Winter Creek

Toward winter's end we half-doubt them,
we forget to keep watch,
and always the first
is a sweet surprise,
in the margins of our wooded acre
where we dig no beds.
Three thin white petals
on three broad leaves
on a stem just strong enough,
in clusters and single
beneath the great firs,
shining softly in slight rain.
What we forget
the trillium remember,
and what, really, did we doubt?
Ourselves, I guess—
our own uncertain stems
and shallow roots,
here where we landed
eighteen years ago
with plans, plantings,
and more years behind us,
likely, than ahead.
True to our species,
we have been slow learners.
We will never know more than a little
of the poem that is this place,
but every spring
the trillium tell us
we have not yet failed it.
What the dark earth wants to say
still rises, still
speaks its silence
in the shade of the spiring trees—

fragile, entire,
and fierce as the furious stars
that gave it birth.
The gift arrives unbidden,
as we arrived to this land
and arrived to each other
and to life itself.
If we work with care,
if we watch and listen
with our flawed faith,
if we honor the mystery
to which we belong
but which does not belong to us,
then we know ourselves
as part of the gift
and may speak its name.
What but love
can raise the trillium
from the cold March earth,
and what but love can be our answer?

Cinders and Flowers

The north side of Mount St. Helens gapes wide open
where it blew out in 1980
and left this scrabbly strew
of gray and white pumice
glaring in afternoon sun
and crunching beneath my bootsteps.
Ten years before the mountain exploded,
I stood on the snowy summit
one summer afternoon
and shouted my joy
down to the expansive earth.
Since then I have earned
an unhappy back,
an ankle that pains me with every step,
a titanium knee, a shoulder
of bone rubbing bone.
Please tell me, believers
in the resurrection of the body—
which one?
Oh, I'd take again the youthful version
were he offered—though not
if his angst and confusions came with him—
and I'm pretty sure
this creaking frame could bear me up the mountain
to search him out.
But why?
That peak where he stood and hollered,
wanting nothing that was not there,
is not there.
The blowout left him
and the forty years between us
in windy space,
a quarter-mile above the crater rim.
If that boy is to live again

he will have to do it
down here,
in this body of complaints
trekking a blasted plain,
a country born dead
but not dead now.
Gophers swam up from their havens, stirring
the grit and pebbles.
Bunchgrasses sunk roots.
Willows, shrubs, and saplings,
sparrows and flycatchers nesting among them,
have taken hold
by the snowmelt stream
that pours from the mountain's core.
And now, this late July,
riots of blossoms have exploded all over —
blue lupine, penstemons
pink and purple,
Indian paintbrush of the deepest orange,
in clumps where I walk
and hazing the farther slopes in soft pastels.
I'm glad I stood
on that summit once, if indeed it was me,
but where, on a mountaintop,
are the birds and flowers?
I'm happy enough to saunter along in my gimpy way
here below,
where I see not as far
but stand in scale
with small beauties making the most of their moment,
my legion of pains
never failing to report
that like the mountain I am alive and finding my way.

Solitude

Never still, mist
drifting the canyon
in luminous veils
opens there, now
there, revealing
green firs as if
just born, dewy
with their own creation,
and closes again
in slow gray swirls.

But nothing, nothing
is revealed, to me
or to any eye
of earth or heaven,
because what
can be hidden?
The great land lives
openly in its seclusion.
The river flows
in whispers, mist
swirls, trees vanish
and trees return —
where they were
and always were
and were never at all,
where they will
and will not be.

Now,
where the mist opens,
atop one tall tree
a raven lights
and tries its voices.

Notes

"For the Fire": This poem owes a debt to George Venn's "Split Kindling," in *Off the Main Road* (Portland: Prescott Street Press, 1978).

"The Sound of Mountain Water": As Wallace Stegner remarked to me, "You stole that title."

"A Year among the Owls": In the early 1980s, Great Horned Owls nested in the Stanford University inner quad.

"Naming the New One": For an alternate account of this scene see Genesis 2:19-20.

"To Mount St. Helens": The school children of La Grande, Oregon — where I was working as a poet in the schools when St. Helens erupted — helped me to see the mountain's joy, as did Ursula Le Guin in her essay, "A Very Warm Mountain."

"The Canyon Wren": The phrase "trick of quiet" I've borrowed from Sherwood Anderson by way of Wallace Stegner. Anderson wrote in a letter to Waldo Frank: "I can remember old fellows in my home town speaking feelingly of an evening spent on the big empty plains. It had taken the shrillness out of them. They had learned the trick of quiet . . ." Stegner quotes this passage in his "Wilderness Letter."

"Opal Creek": The Opal Creek watershed is home to the largest remaining stand of old-growth forest in the Oregon Cascades, with many trees 500 to 1,000 years old. Parts of the drainage had long been slated for timber sales by the U. S. Forest Service when the area finally received wilderness protection in 1996.

"The European Birch": The poet Denise Levertov, a native of England, lived in the eastern United States for most of her life before moving, in 1989, to Seattle, where she would spend her last years. It was a walk with her in the rainy Seattle streets that inspired this poem. I knew her from the 1980s at Stanford, where she was one of my teachers.

"The Gray Whales Passing Point Reyes": Charles Scammon was one of the captains who hunted the California gray whale almost to extinction near the end of the 19th century. The whales, now protected by law, appear to be thriving again.

"A Candle in Solitude": This poem and two others—"Christmas Psalm in Solitude" and "Solitude"—stem from a four-and-a-half-month stay in the Rogue River backcountry, isolated from human company, in the winter of 2000–2001. "The River" came out of a later stay in the same place.

"Poem for Fern Ridge Library": When my local library was renovated and expanded in 1999, I was commissioned to write a poem to run as a continuous single-line frieze on the upper walls around the main interior spaces of the new building. My guidelines were to create something accessible to both children and adults and to incorporate the seasons and some of the natural history of our region.

"If, Like Me, You Are Not an Oregon Native but Wish You Were." Section 4: "Filbert" is the common Northwest name for the hazelnut, which is grown widely in western Oregon. Section 7: Oregon is one of five states that don't impose a sales tax. Sales tax measures are routinely proposed and routinely voted down by the state legislature or the electorate.

"The Wind in Sand Creek Canyon": T.H. Watkins—historian, conservation writer, lover of the American West—was for many years the editor of *Wilderness* magazine, formerly published by The Wilderness Society. He gave me my start as a magazine essayist and environmental journalist, and later took me on as poetry editor.

"In the Ancient Bristlecone Pine Forest": Individual bristlecone pines live as long as 4,700 years. The White Mountains are in east central California, between Owens Valley and the Nevada line.

"For a Wedding under Mount Adams": Written for the wedding of Caressa Gullikson and Geoff Houghton, June 21, 1993.

Acknowledgments

Jim Hepworth of Confluence Press published *Common Ground*—my first book of poems and first book of any kind—in 1988, and has kept it in print ever since. I thank him for that faithfulness, for his generous permission to reprint poems from *Common Ground*, and also for the clear eye he cast on those and on the new poems as well. And I thank him for his friendship.

Due acknowledgment is made to Salmon Run Press, which published *All Things Touched by Wind* in 1994.

•

I thank, again, the editors and publishers of the following magazines, where many of the poems in *Common Ground* and *All Things Touched by Wind* first appeared in print:

The Amicus Journal, Calapooya Collage, Clearwater Journal, CutBank, Earth First, Fireweed, High Country News, ISLE, Kentucky Poetry Review, North American Review, Northern Lights, Not Man Apart, Oregon East, Orion, Petroglyph, Poetry, Poetry Now, Seattle Review, Sequoia, Sierra, Snapdragon, South Dakota Review, The Southern Review, Southwest Review, Wild Oregon, Writers' Forum, and *Zone 3.*

Of the new poems, some appeared or are forthcoming in the following magazines:

Audubon: "The River," in prose as "The Flow of Life"

Bloomsbury Review: "The Wind in Sand Creek Canyon"

ISLE: Interdisciplinary Studies in Literature and Environment: "The Canyon"

LBJ: Literary Bird Journal: "Blue Heron in the Cloverleaf" and "To a Friend Who Doubts That Her Writing Matters"

Portland Magazine: "Christmas Psalm in Solitude"

Reed Magazine: "Poem for Fern Ridge Library" and "To a Reed College Sophomore Soon to Drop Out, Fall 1967"

Terrain.org: "Cinders and Flowers" and "The Barn"

Texas Observer: "Spring Burning"

The Oregonian: "Blowout"

·

Some of the poems both old and new have been anthologized as follows, often in earlier form:

"The Longing": *The Pushcart Prize VIII: Best of the Small Presses,* edited by Bill Henderson. Wainscott, New York: Pushcart Press, 1983.

"Of Earth" and "A Year among the Owls": *The Uncommon Touch: Fiction and Poetry from the Stanford Writing Workshop,* edited by John L'Heureux. Stanford University: Stanford Alumni Association, 1989.

"Common Ground" and "Descendants of the Nuclear Age": *The Forgotten Language: Contemporary Poets and Nature,* edited by Christopher Merrill. Salt Lake City: Peregrine Smith Books, 1991.

"Dependence Day": *From Here We Speak: An Anthology of Oregon Poetry,* edited by Ingrid Wendt and Primus St. John. Corvallis: Oregon State University Press, 1993.

"Naming the New One": *Northern Lights,* edited by Deborah Clow and Donald Snow. New York: Vintage, 1994.

"Unbound" and "To Mt. St. Helens": *Poetry of the American West,* edited by Alison Hawthorne Deming. New York: Columbia University Press, 1996.

"Spring Burning": *Wild Song: Poems of the Natural World,* edited by John Daniel. Athens: University of Georgia Press, 1998.

"The Canyon" and "The Canyon Wren": *Getting Over the Color Green: Contemporary Environmental Literature of the Southwest,* edited by Scott Slovic. Tucson: University of Arizona Press, 2001.

·

"Poem for Fern Ridge Library" was originally published in 1999 as a 274-foot stenciled frieze along the walls of the main interior spaces of Fern Ridge Library in Veneta, Oregon. The design, lettering, and art work were done, beautifully, by Marilyn Reaves and Carol Chapel.

"Dependence Day" was printed as a broadside by Mad River Press in Richmond, Massachusetts.

"Poem for Fern Ridge Library" and "Dependence Day" were printed as broadsides by the inestimable Sandy Tilcock of lone goose press in Eugene, Oregon.

"A Prayer among Friends" was printed as a broadside by my generous friends Carolyn Servid and Dorik Mechau of the Island Institute in Sitka, Alaska.

"Blowout" was printed as a broadside by Keegan Meegan Press & Bindery in Portland.

•

I am deeply grateful to the entire Roger and Karen Hamilton clan, for allowing me to squat on their ranch and raise some poems amid their hay, cattle, pigs, and children, and a special nod to Andy and Gabe for making the Pine Flat cottage a home.

My thanks to the board, staff, and founders of Playa, on Summer Lake in the Oregon high desert, for a six-week residency in the spring of 2011 during which I got much done on this manuscript. Playa is a wonderful place to be and to write.

John Laursen read the prose parts of the book, to their benefit, and Tanya Berry contributed the resurrection-of-the-body punchline in "Cinders and Flowers."

Five poets encouraged and helped me in distinct ways very early, when I most needed encouragement and help. I thank Patricia Henley, Ona Siporin, George Venn, Wendell Berry, and the memory of William Stafford.

Great thanks to Sam Rooeintan, who made his painting available for the cover, and to Christine Holbert of Lost Horse Press for designing a beautiful book, inside and out.

Lastly and firstly, I am grateful to Marilyn Matheson Daniel for the fine madness that persuaded her to marry a poet.